W9-CEX-981

Boogie-Woogie Bugs Activity Book

Songs and Activities

By Don Cooper

Illustrated by Sandra Forrest

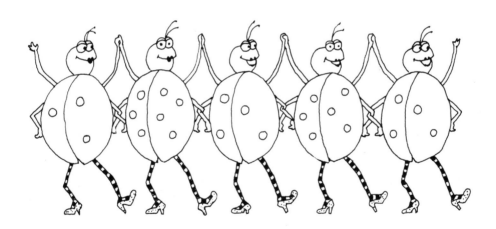

Random House New York

Copyright © 1989 by Random House, Inc. All rights reserved under International and
Pan-American Copyright Conventions. Published in the United States by Random House, Inc.,
New York, and simultaneously in Canada by Random House of Canada Limited, Toronto.
ISBN: 0-394-82950-6

Lyrics copyright © 1989 by New Mutant Music. Illustrations © 1989 by Sandra Forrest.
All rights reserved. Manufactured in the United States of America   1 2 3 4 5 6 7 8 9 0

Boogie-Woogie Bugs

Outside in the garden there's a party going on.
Late at night, when you are tucked in bed,
The bugs all get together
To dance to their favorite songs.
The cornstalk bends an ear,
And the lettuce bobs its head.
The mosquito's buzzin' on the slide trombone,
While the spider keeps the beat,
Snapping out the rhythm in the snap-bean rows
With his eight long legs and feet,
And the crickets chirp out a sweet soul chorus
Underneath the summer sky.
It's a real humdinger,
'Cause the spotlight singer is Madame Butterfly!

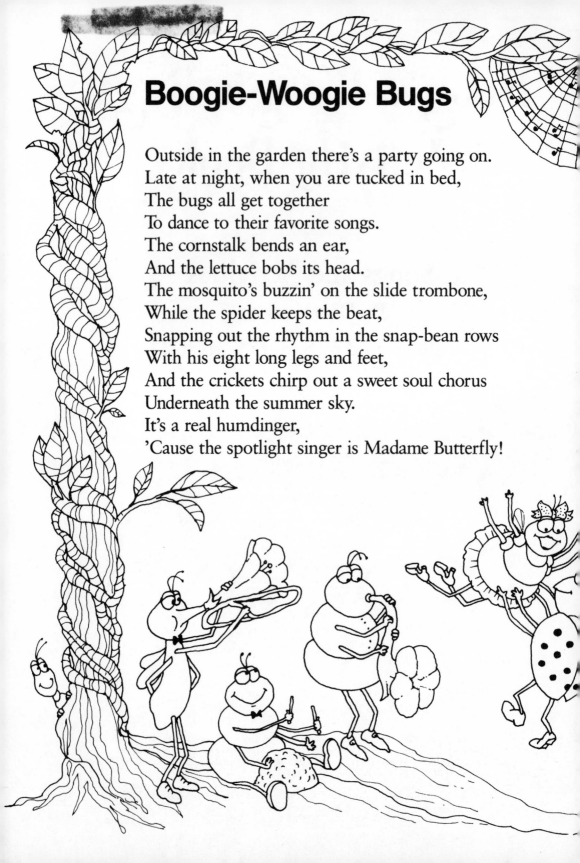

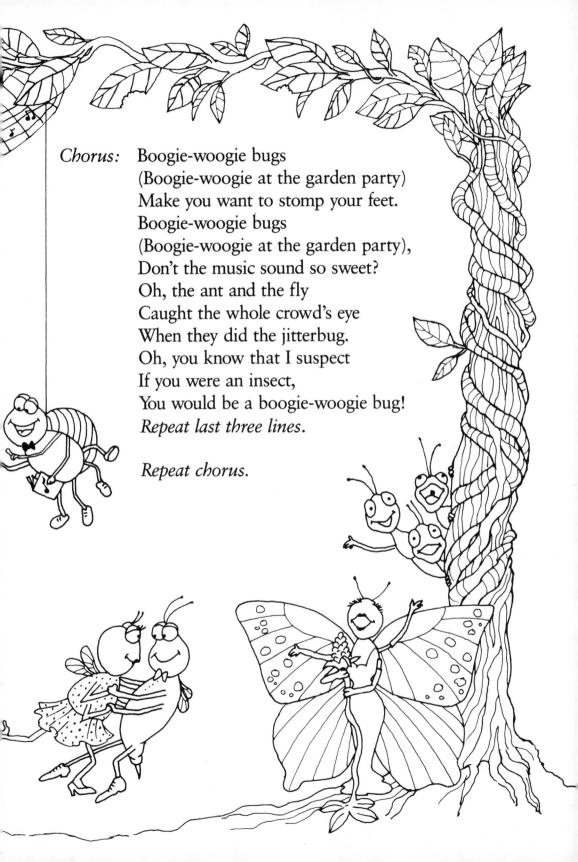

Chorus: Boogie-woogie bugs
        (Boogie-woogie at the garden party)
        Make you want to stomp your feet.
        Boogie-woogie bugs
        (Boogie-woogie at the garden party),
        Don't the music sound so sweet?
        Oh, the ant and the fly
        Caught the whole crowd's eye
        When they did the jitterbug.
        Oh, you know that I suspect
        If you were an insect,
        You would be a boogie-woogie bug!
        Repeat last three lines.

        Repeat chorus.

Little Problems

There are 4,000 different kinds of ladybugs. One of the differences is the number of spots on their backs. Count the spots on the ladybugs below and circle the two ladybugs that are the same!

All ladybugs have six legs. Draw the correct number of legs on the ladybug below.

Ladybug, Ladybug

Chorus: Ladybug, ladybug, fly away home,
It's light and the sky is blue.
Ladybug, ladybug, fly away home,
Your children are waiting for you.
Oh, ladybug, ladybug, fly away home,
Night's falling and daytime is through.
Wave me good-bye and then fly away home,
'Cause I've got to hurry home too.
Wave me good-bye and then fly away home,
'Cause I've got to hurry, hey, I've got to fly away,
I've got to hurry home too.

Lovely little ladybug, upon your purple flower,
This clover field must seem real big to you.
In your polka-dotted gown,
You while away the hours,
But you've got more important things to do.
In school I learned a nursery rhyme
About you and I know
That you are running out of time,
It's time for you to go!

Repeat chorus.

Even though bees can sting and be a nuisance, they can also be very helpful to people. If they didn't carry pollen from plant to plant, we wouldn't have many of the fruits and flowers that we enjoy. Honeybees are some of the most helpful insects. We eat their honey and make candles from the wax of their honeycombs.

Honeybee

When spring arrives, the warm sun shines
And the beehive starts a-buzzin'.
The queen bee's in her bedroom,
Waking from her winter sleep.
The worker bees all rub their eyes
And they lick their lips, because
When the last dewdrop has fallen,
It's sweet pollen they will seek.
All the boy bees comb their hairs
And spread their wings.
When they line up in a beeline,
You can hear those drones all singing...

Chorus: Won't you be my honey, honey,
Won't you be my queen bee.
'Neath the sun we'll fly and hum,
Around and in between the
Brightly colored blossoms,
On the flowers and the trees.
Be my love, we'll live our lives
And raise a hive of honeybees.
My love, we'll live our lives
And raise a hive of honeybees.

Oh, the workers travel far from home
To fill their little bellies
With flower nectar.
Then they store some pollen on their legs,
Which they take back to the honeycomb
To make beebread and royal jelly,
While the cleaning bees clean up the room
Where the queen will lay her eggs.
All the boy bees wait to see what fate will bring.
When the eggs hatch out new baby queens,
You can hear those drones all singing...

Repeat chorus.

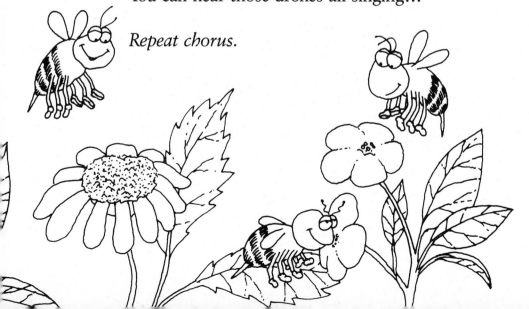

The Alphabug

This riddle's delight
Is an insect in flight.
It's as easy as 1–2–3.
When is a bug
Like a letter you write?
The answer is
When it's A __ __ __!

To find the answer to this rhyming riddle, circle every third letter below, as we've already done with the A, then fill in the blanks with the circled letters!

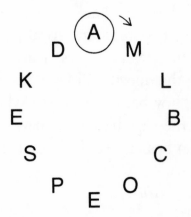

Now draw a picture of this "alphabug"!

Beelines

Worker bees collect nectar from the flowers. When they have collected enough, they fly back to their hive. The path that they take is called a beeline. Find the seven hidden bees and draw a beeline from each one to the hive. (We've already done one for you as an example.)

A Baby Bumblebee

(Traditional)
Adapted by Don Cooper

I'm bringing home a baby bumblebee.
Won't my mama be so proud of me?
I'm bringing home a baby bumblebee...
Ouch! It stung me!

I'm bringing home a dandy dragonfly.
Won't my dad be very glad that I am
Bringing home a dandy dragonfly...
Yeoww! It stuck me!

I'm bringing home a nasty little gnat,
Bet my sis will be so happy that
I'm bringing home a nasty little gnat...
Eek! It bit me!

I'm bringing home a creeping cock-a-roach.
Bet my brother thinks it's just a joke!
I'm bringing home a creeping cock-a-roach...
Yikes! It scared me!

I'm bringing home a bunch of buggy friends.
Guess my family will be happy when
I bring them home a bunch of buggy friends...
Hey, where's everybody going?

The Crazy Collector

This collector is trying to catch bugs to take home to study, but he's doing it in a pretty crazy way. Find five things in the picture below that the collector is doing wrong.

Buggie Burgers

I'm making a web, I'm weaving it tight,
I'm going to catch a fat ol' fly for dinner tonight!
From corner to corner I'm weaving my thread,
Any fly will be a goner who bumps into my web.
Well, don't get me wrong,
I'm no meany—matter of fact,
I'm just a hungry spider
Lookin' for a midnight snack!

Chorus: Oooh, oooh, I love them buggie burgers,
Crispy moths and flies.
They're a treat made for a spider,
Any shape or any size.
I love to see them buggie burgers
Caught up in my web.
You can keep your beans,
Just give me buggie burgers instead!
Keep your beans and greens,
Just give me buggie burgers instead.

Yum, yum, chomp, chomp, my oh my,
I'm so hungry I could eat a horse...fly!
I don't want no baked potata,
I'd rather eat a sweet cicada.
Well, gnats make dandy spider snacks,
But a fly tastes even greater!

I'm making a web, it's a spider's delight,
I got eight busy legs and a big appetite.
If I'm lucky, some fuzzy moth, drawn by the light,
Might poke his head into my web
And stick around for a bite.
Oh, don't get me wrong,
I'm no meany—matter of fact,
I'm just a hungry spider
Lookin' for a midnight snack!

Repeat chorus.

Now kids, don't you eat bugs;
Stick to your bread and apple cider.
But a buggie burger's what you need
To feed a hungry spider.
Yum, yum, buggie burgers,
One of my favorite dishes (BURP!).
Pardon me, but my oh my,
That fly was sure delicious!

A Webster's Alphabet

You may have heard of a spelling bee—well, here's a
spelling spider! Connect the dots in order, from A to Z,
and help the spider build its web.

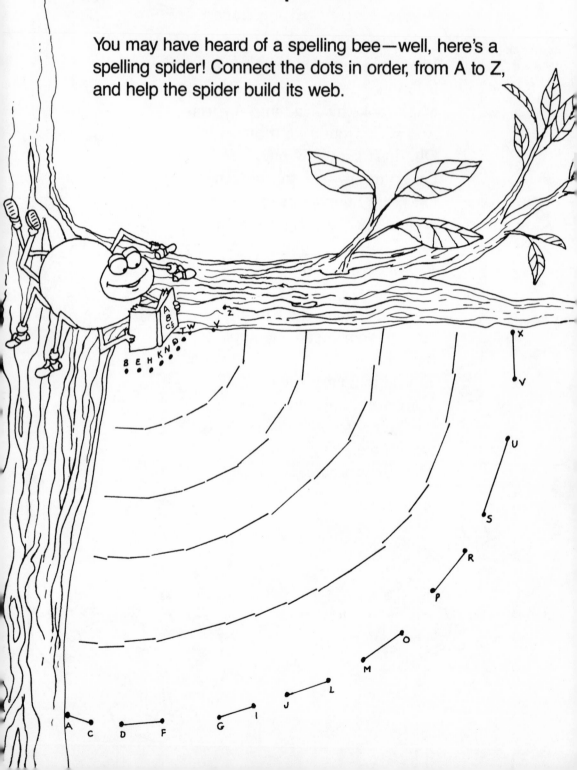

The Itsy, Bitsy Spider

(Traditional) Adapted by Don Cooper

Chorus: The itsy, bitsy spider went up the waterspout.
Down came the rain
And washed the spider out.
Out came the sun
And dried up all the rain.
So the itsy, bitsy spider went up the spout again!

The itsy, bitsy spider crawled up my mama's leg,
It sat down right beside her—
"Please go away!" she begged.
The spider didn't move till
Mama jumped about.
So the itsy, bitsy spider went up the waterspout!

The itsy, bitsy spider climbed up on Daddy's chair.
It crawled across his shoulder
And up into his hair.
Its prickly legs were tickly,
So Daddy plucked him out.
So the itsy, bitsy spider went up the waterspout!

The itsy, bitsy spider climbed up into my bed.
It nestled on the pillow
Beside my sleepy head.
It crawled into my nose,
And I sneezed and blew it out.
So the itsy, bitsy spider went up the waterspout!

Repeat chorus.

Finders Keepers!

If you're going to collect bugs, you must know where to look. Different bugs can be found in different places. Draw a line from each bug to the place where you're most likely to find it.

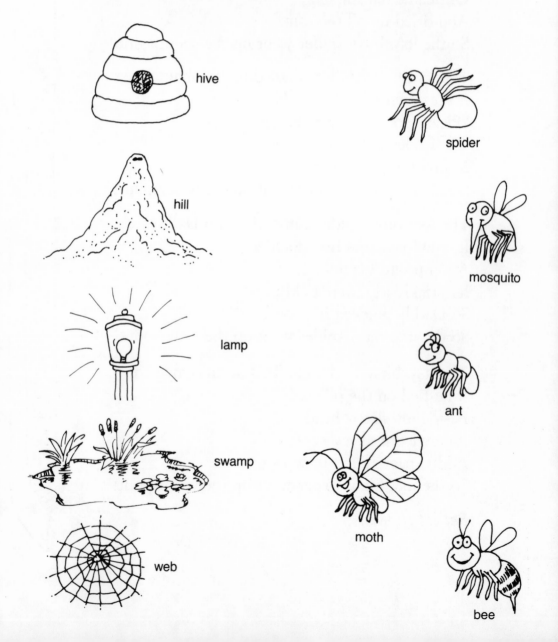

hive

spider

hill

mosquito

lamp

ant

swamp

moth

web

bee

A Buzzle

Question: What did one mosquito say to the other when it wanted to be left alone?

Answer:

,

__ __ __ __   __ __ __   __ __!

In our secret code each symbol stands for a letter of the alphabet. Use the code breaker below and fill in the right letters to find the answer.

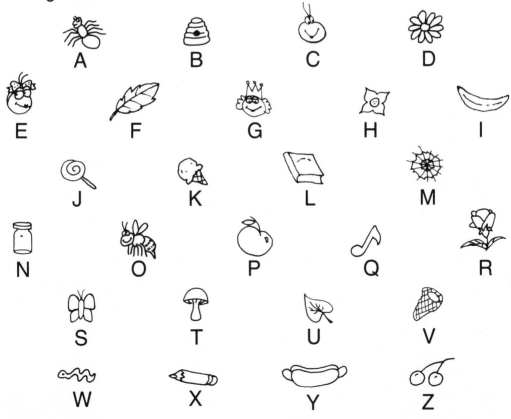

A B C D

E F G H I

J K L M

N O P Q R

S T U V

W X Y Z

Skeeter Bites

Skeeter bites, skeeter bites,
Buzzin' in the woods at night.
Button up your jammies tight,
The skeeter bites are comin'!
Skeeter bites, skeeter bites,
Buzzin' in your room at night.
Honey, jump beneath the covers,
'Fore the skeeters bite your bum!

Chorus: Buzz, buzz, buzz. *(Repeat.)*

Skeeter bites, skeeter bites,
Little bumps so red and bright.
Make you want to twitch and itch
Just listenin' to them hum!
Skeeter bites, skeeter bites,
Like an orchestra in flight.
Honey, jump beneath the covers,
'Fore the skeeters bite your bum!

Repeat chorus.

They got them little skeeter noses,
When they poke you, how it stings!
Got them wiry little leggies,
Got them hummin' little wings.
They all come buzzin' 'round
When the weather's gettin' hot,
So jump beneath your covers
Just to show them that you're not for biting!

Repeat first verse.

Shine, Little Firefly, Shine

Chorus: Light my way to the Milky Way,
Give me a twinkling sign.
Grant the wish that I wish today,
And shine, little firefly, shine.

In the summertime when the sun goes down,
Outside in the darkening sky,
God's little candles fly around,
The sparkling fireflies.

Repeat chorus.

First you make a wish on a firefly,
Which you've caught in the palm of your hand.
When you let it go, if it starts to glow,
Your wish may come true, my friend!

Repeat chorus.

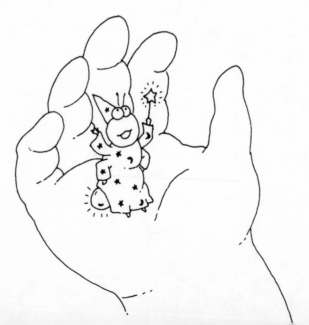

Egg-citing Insects!

Here are some ways that you can create make-believe bugs out of egg cartons and pipe cleaners!

1. A caterpillar:
Cut the top or bottom of an empty egg carton in half, lengthwise. Poke two holes in the front and insert a pipe cleaner in each hole for antennas. Decorate the caterpillar with paints or crayons.

2. A spider:
Cut out two egg-carton segments. Attach eight pipe cleaner "legs" to the rear segment. Decorate as you like. If you want, you can create a "web" of string inside a shoebox for your spider to sit on.

3. A ladybug:
Cut out one egg-carton segment. Attach six short pipe cleaner legs to the body. Color the ladybug red, then add two black dots for eyes and bigger black dots on its back.

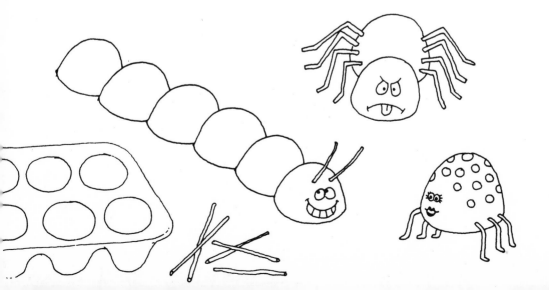

Down on the Ant Farm

Well, just beyond your window
Or right outside your door,
Behind your kitchen counter
Or underneath your floor,
If you get down on your hands and knees
And look real closely, you might see
A farm with barns and cows and plants,
A colony, a farm of ants!

Chorus: Hey, down on the ant farm things are hopping,
They're milking ant cows, planting crops.
And if you watch them, you'll agree,
The ants are much like you and me.
They're gathering food, they're building towers—
Hey, I could watch these ants for hours.
They work to help their family,
The ants are just like you and me.

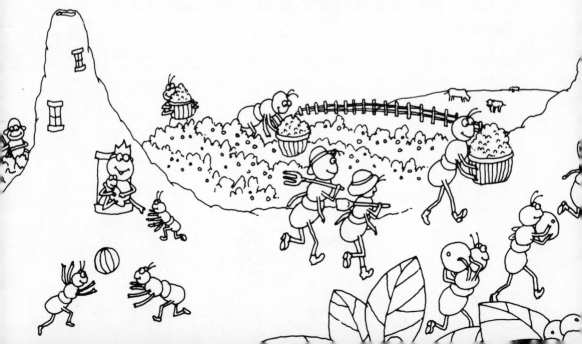

There are soldier ants who guard the door
Against their enemies,
And work ants hauling rice to store
Up in the granaries.
Others tend to the queen and her babies—jeepers!—
They've even got pets and ant housekeepers,
Collecting honeydew like bees
And growing mushrooms 'neath the leaves.

Hey, down on the ant farm ants are working,
All together, no one's shirking.
You'll rarely see such industry,
The ants are much like you and me.
They feed their hungry, heal their sickly,
Get things done, together, quickly.
They share and share alike you see,
The ants are just like you and me.
Cooperation is the key,
The ants are just like you and me!

A-Hunting He Will Go
(An Amazing Adventure)

Ants work hard, and they work together, just like people. Soldier ants guard the doors, cleaning ants clean the colony, and worker ants not only build the anthills but go out and hunt for food. One place you may have seen ants hunting for food is on a family picnic. Help this worker ant find his way up to the picnic, where he can pick up some tasty crumbs.

The Fuzzy Caterpillar

A fuzzy little caterpillar
Sat upon a leaf.
He thought he'd munch a bit of lunch
To try and stem his grief.
He felt so tiny, slow and spiny,
Breathing out a sigh,
He chewed his greens and dreamed his dreams
Of floating through the sky.

Someday real soon my own cocoon
Will hang beneath the sun,
And I will sleep, safe in the keep
Of the bed which I have spun.
In sleep I know my wings will grow,
And when the time is nigh,
I'll break the threads of my soft bed
And float into the sky.

Chorus: And they'll say, Was he fuzzy?
Was he just a worm this high?
How can it be that such as he
Can be a butterfly? Fly away!

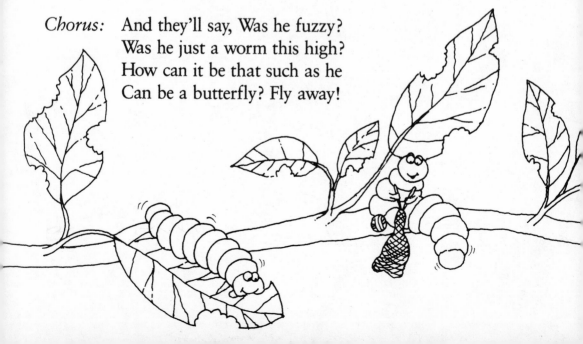

Remembering well this wondrous tale
He'd heard since his first day,
He snacked his snack, then arched his back
And crawled along his way.
Before he'd gone an inch along
He heard a magic tune,
And in time to that mysterious song
He started his cocoon!

He wove it like a magic coat
And hung it on a thread,
And at the music's closing note
He slipped into his bed.
The days they flew, his wings they grew,
The nights were long and cold.
His fuzzy shape became a cape
Of colors bright and bold! Fly away!

He slept and grew the winter through,
And then one special day,
He spread his wings to greet the spring
And proudly flew away!

Repeat chorus twice.

Fly Away!

The cocoon below has just opened up. Connect the dots from 1 to 20 to see what came out of it, then color and decorate the shape you've made!

Other Bug Games and Activities

1. A bug buzzer:
Fold a piece of tissue paper over a pocket comb. Place your lips against it lightly and hum through your lips to make a bug buzzer!

2. A spider web collection:
With the help of an adult, spray a spider web with a light coating of hair spray or clear lacquer. While it is still wet, place a sheet of black construction paper against it from behind. When the web attaches itself to the paper, spray it once more to permanently stick it.

3. Growing a butterfly:
Collect a caterpillar along with the twig and leaf it's on. Put them in a jar. Cover the bottom of the jar with sand or gravel, and include a small container of water to put new twigs and leaves in. This will keep the caterpillar's food supply fresh. Cover the top of the jar with cheesecloth or aluminum foil with holes punched in it to let air through. Set the jar near a window, but not in direct sunlight. Watch the caterpillar spin its cocoon, and wait for the butterfly to come out. When it does, enjoy its beauty, then let it fly away!

4. The fireflies spell your name!
Write your name lightly in pencil on a piece of black construction paper. With the pencil point or a pen point poke holes along the letters you've written. Hang the paper on a lampshade or hold a flashlight behind it in a dark room and pretend the fireflies are spelling your name in the darkening sky.

Do the Bug

If you feel a little blue,
Kind of glum and out of sorts,
When you've got that itchy feeling
'Cause the day has got you bored,
Call on your imagination,
Make believe, pretend, and play.
You're in luck, listen up—
Here's how to chase those blues away...

Chorus: Do the bug, do the bug,
It's a dance, it's a game,
You can make believe that
You're a bug of any name!
Do the bug, do the bug,
It's a lot of fun to play.
If you're glum, do the bug
And your blues will fly away!
If you're glum, do the bug
And your blues will fly away!

Make believe that you're a caterpillar
Wiggling 'round the room,
Then wrap a blanket 'round you
And pretend it's your cocoon.
When you open up the blanket,
Raise your hands up to the sky
And flap your arms about
Like a happy butterfly!